CREATIVE LOG SCULPTURE

CREATIVE LOG SCULPTURE

John Matthews 1933-

Drake Publishers Inc   New York

ISBN 87749-250-6

Library of Congress Catalog Card No. 72-1257

Published in 1972 by
Drake Publishers Inc
381 Park Avenue South
New York, N.Y. 10016
© John Matthews 1972

Printed in Great Britain

PREFACE

Creative Log Sculpture is not beyond anyone, at any age, with the will to try.

Primitive man probably practised this type of carving to produce weapons for defence and hunting, crude canoes, simple constructions and furniture, and objects of pleasure which represented the things around him. The need to make individual items for creative pleasure is still with us, and log sculpture can be extremely satisfying in this age of artificial materials and mass production. It also helps to develop powers of observation, appreciation of the beauties of this natural material, and the art of bringing movement and life to sketches and carvings.

Basic work can be done by adult beginners at evening institutes, art schools, technical schools or at home, and by quite young school children. The tools and the techniques for their use are generally simple and require little initial skill, and a reasonable standard can be attained in a very short time.

The raw material is cheap and available in most districts for the good-mannered asking. Suitable branches for working are usually between $\frac{1}{2}$" and $2\frac{1}{2}$" in diameter. Full use of colour, texture, knot positions and the flow of the grain should be made, and although a smooth surface is usually most suitable, bark or a gouged surface can sometimes be extremely effective. Generally, a natural finish looks better than a polished one.

This book aims to present the subject in a simple pictorial manner. It is arranged in four sections with a general introduction, photographs and development sketches of log sculpture, a skeleton working guide and details of tools.

The general introduction gives an insight into the process, starting with the selection of possible sculptures in their raw state and continuing through the various working stages to the finished object.

A large section is then devoted to photographs of numerous log sculptures accompanied by development sketches. If these are carefully studied, they will foster an awareness of an enormous range of sculptural subjects, and the many possibilities of the raw material. The various working stages and methods of presentation are also demonstrated. (A signet ring is included in each photograph to indicate the scale of the sculpture.)

Thirdly, there is a skeleton guide which covers the development of log sculpture from the initial selection, through the trimming, shaping and finishing stages, to stand design and production.

Finally there is a small section on suitable tools and their use, together with specifications for ordering.

Abbreviations: M.P.B.—Machine-planed boarding
M.P.S.—Machine-planed scantling

John Matthews

WOOD SUPPLIERS

Woodcraft Supply Corp.
313 Montvale Avenue
Woburn, Massachusetts 01801

Albert Constantine and Sons
2050 Eastchester Road
Bronx, N.Y. 10461

Craftsman Wood Service Co.
2727 South Mary Street
Chicago, Illinois 60608

Minnesota Woodworkers Supply Co.
925 Winnetka Avenue
Minneapolis, Minnesota 55427

CONTENTS

	Page
INTRODUCTION TO CREATIVE LOG SCULPTURE	10
PHOTOGRAPHS AND THEIR DEVELOPMENT DETAILS	12
SKELETON WORKING GUIDE	70
TOOL DETAILS	81

INTRODUCTION TO CREATIVE LOG SCULPTURE

(1)

THIS IS A METHOD FOR DEVELOPING INTERESTING
CREATIVE SCULPTURES FROM LOGS, BRANCHES
AND ROOTS.

(RAW MATERIAL)

(2)

MOST TYPES OF TREES ARE
SUITABLE.

(EXAMPLES)

HAWTHORN   **CHESTNUT**   **SYCAMORE**   **ELM**

APPLE   **BEECH**   **ASH**   **OAK**

(3)

STUDY THE FOLLOWING
PHOTOGRAPHS AND THEIR
DEVELOPMENT SKETCHES.

NOTE

AFTER STUDYING THE PICTURES USE
THE SKELETON WORKING GUIDE
FOLLOWING TO MAKE ORIGINAL
SCULPTURES OF YOUR OWN.

RHINOCEROS
DEVELOPMENT DETAILS

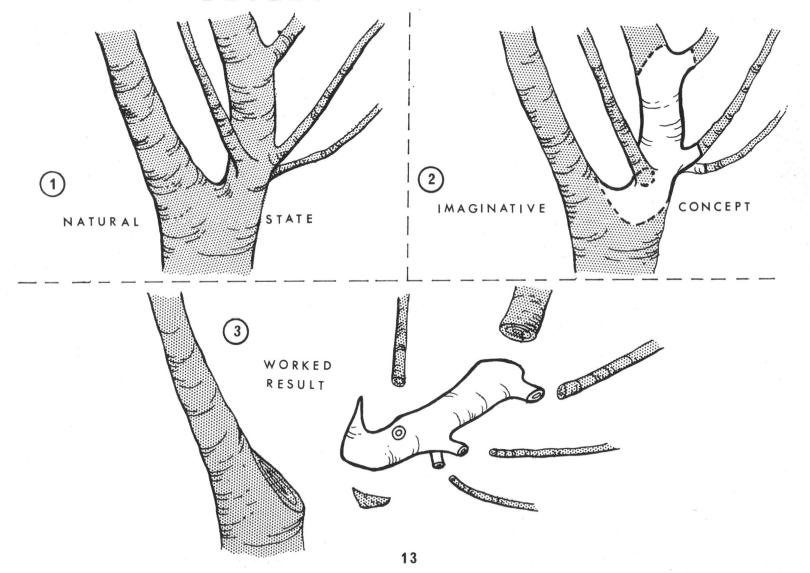

1 NATURAL   STATE

2 IMAGINATIVE   CONCEPT

3 WORKED RESULT

13

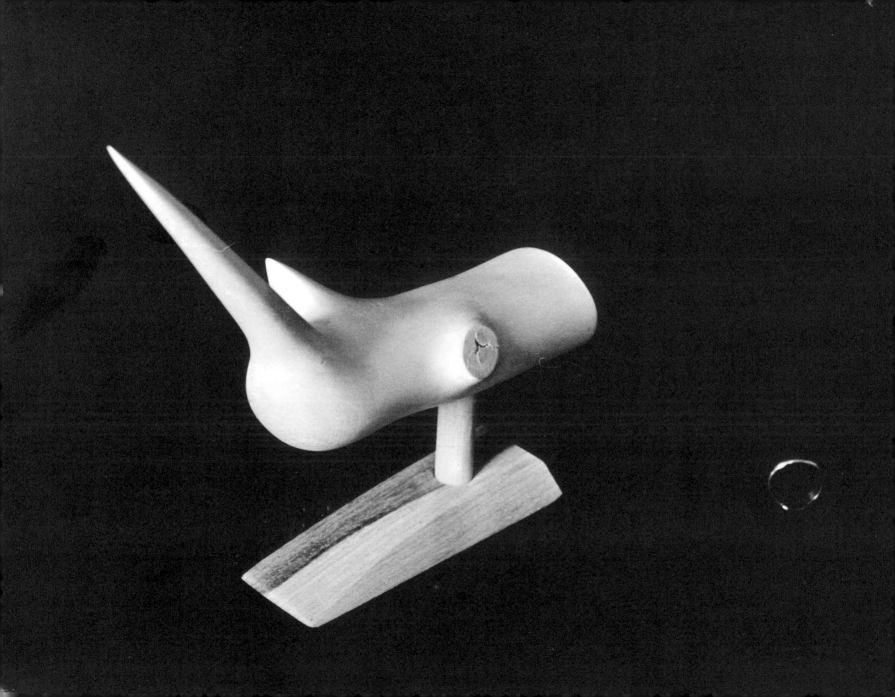

RHINOCEROS'S HEAD
DEVELOPMENT DETAILS

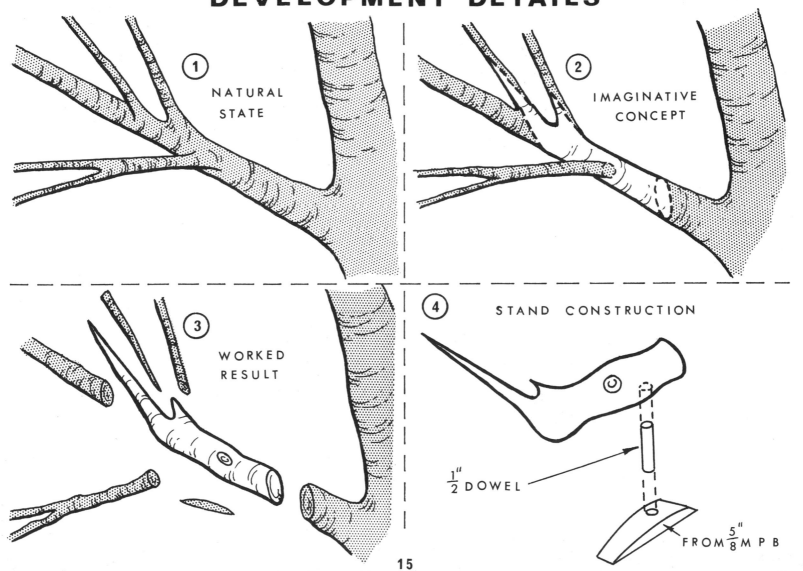

① NATURAL STATE

② IMAGINATIVE CONCEPT

③ WORKED RESULT

④ STAND CONSTRUCTION

$\frac{1}{2}$" DOWEL

FROM $\frac{5}{8}$" M P B

15

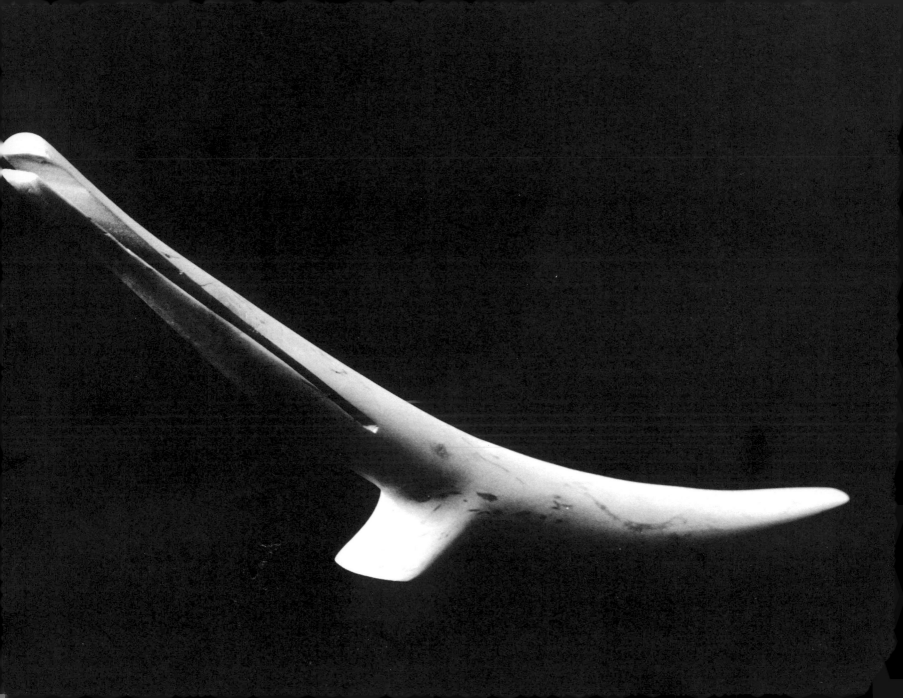

CROCODILE
DEVELOPMENT DETAILS

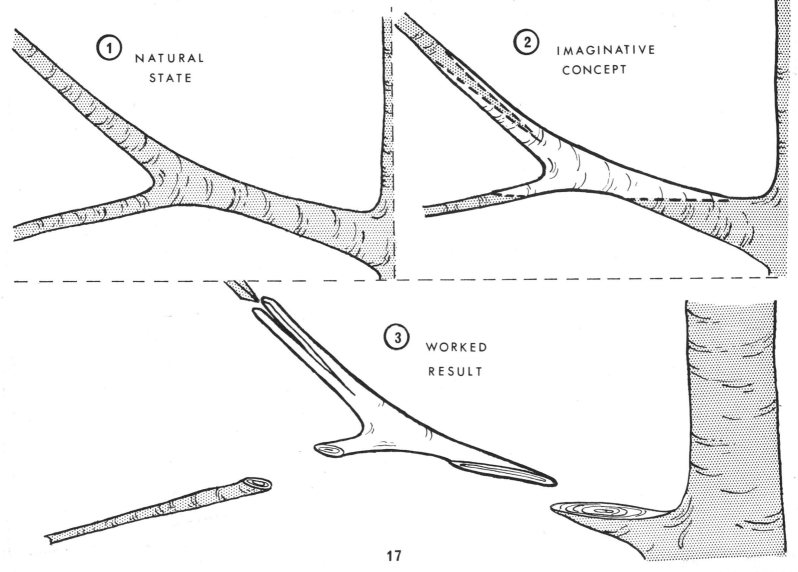

① NATURAL STATE

② IMAGINATIVE CONCEPT

③ WORKED RESULT

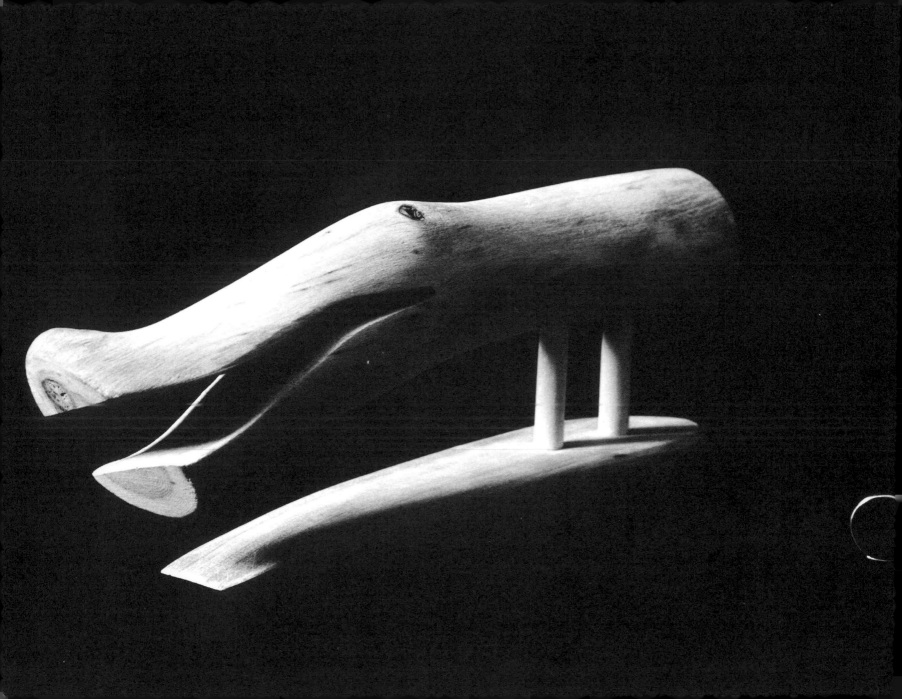

CROCODILE'S HEAD
DEVELOPMENT DETAILS

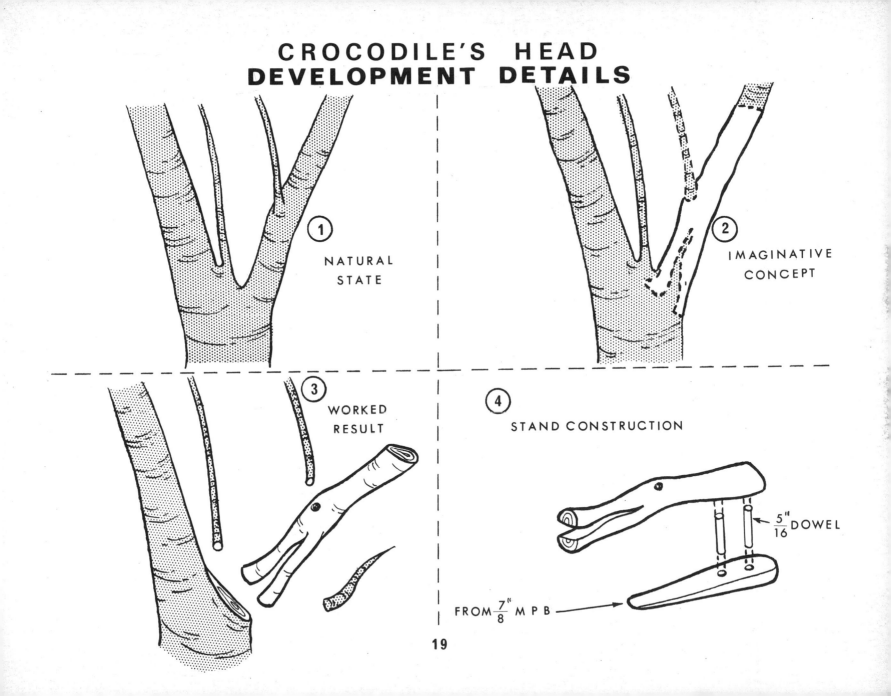

① NATURAL STATE

② IMAGINATIVE CONCEPT

③ WORKED RESULT

④ STAND CONSTRUCTION

$\frac{5"}{16}$ DOWEL

FROM $\frac{7"}{8}$ M P B

19

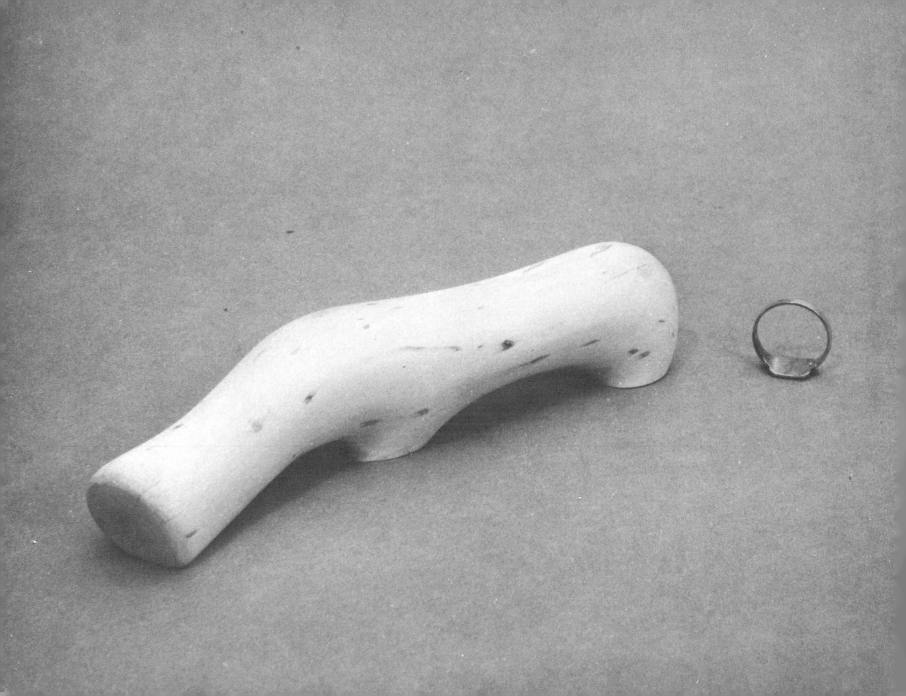

HIPPOPOTAMUS
DEVELOPMENT DETAILS

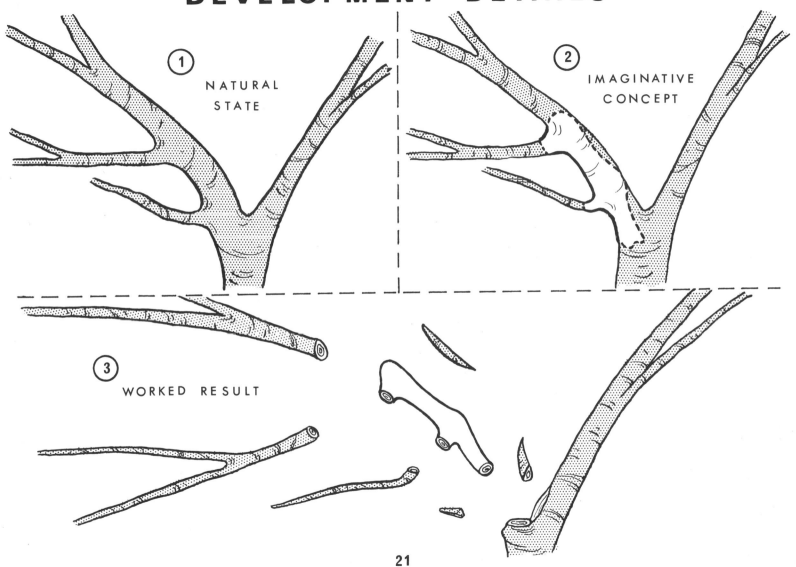

1 NATURAL STATE

2 IMAGINATIVE CONCEPT

3 WORKED RESULT

HIPPOPOTAMUS'S HEAD
DEVELOPMENT DETAILS

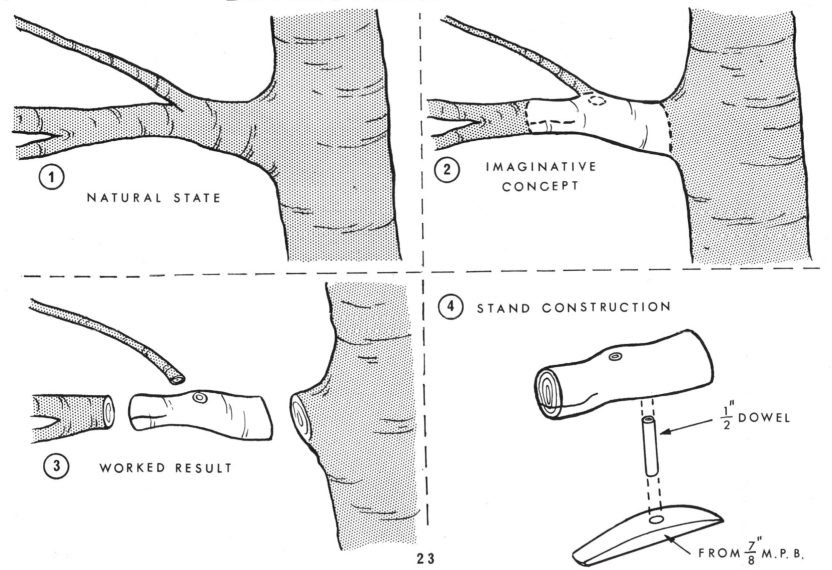

① NATURAL STATE

② IMAGINATIVE CONCEPT

③ WORKED RESULT

④ STAND CONSTRUCTION

$\frac{1}{2}"$ DOWEL

FROM $\frac{7}{8}"$ M.P.B.

ELEPHANT'S HEAD
DEVELOPMENT DETAILS

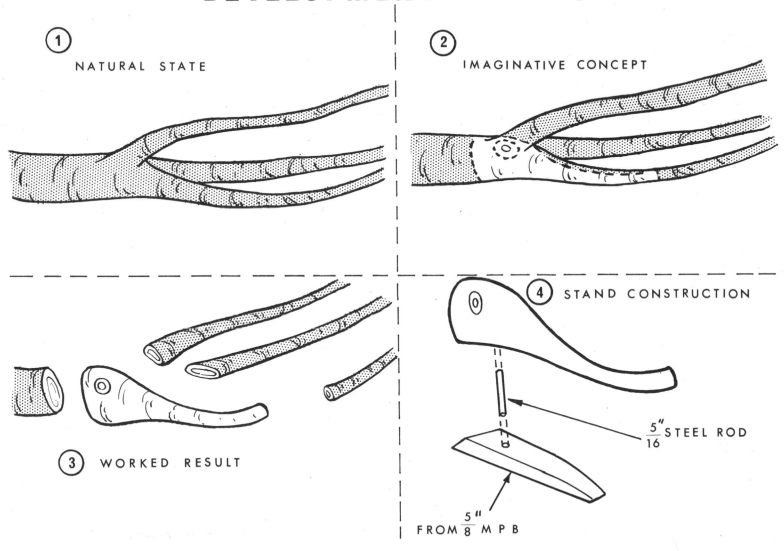

① NATURAL STATE

② IMAGINATIVE CONCEPT

③ WORKED RESULT

④ STAND CONSTRUCTION

$\frac{5}{16}$" STEEL ROD

FROM $\frac{5}{8}$" M P B

LIZARD
DEVELOPMENT DETAILS

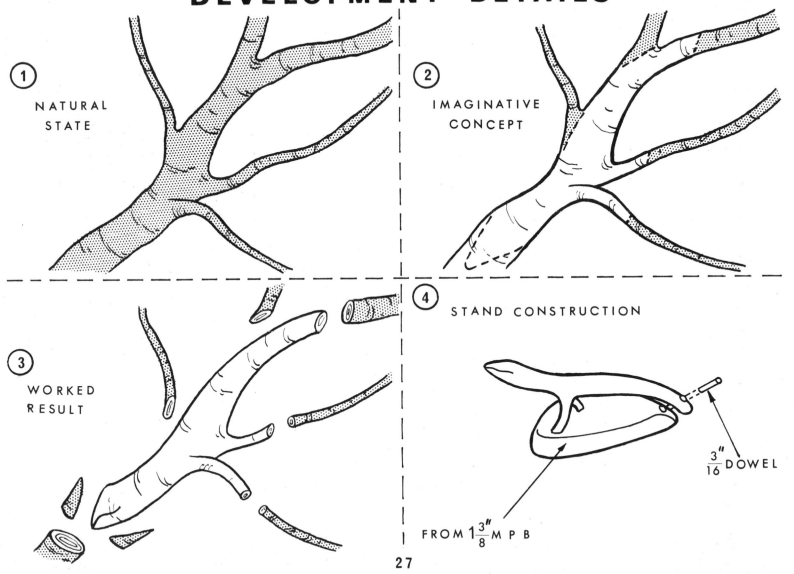

① NATURAL STATE

② IMAGINATIVE CONCEPT

③ WORKED RESULT

④ STAND CONSTRUCTION

$\frac{3''}{16}$ DOWEL

FROM $1\frac{3''}{8}$ M P B

27

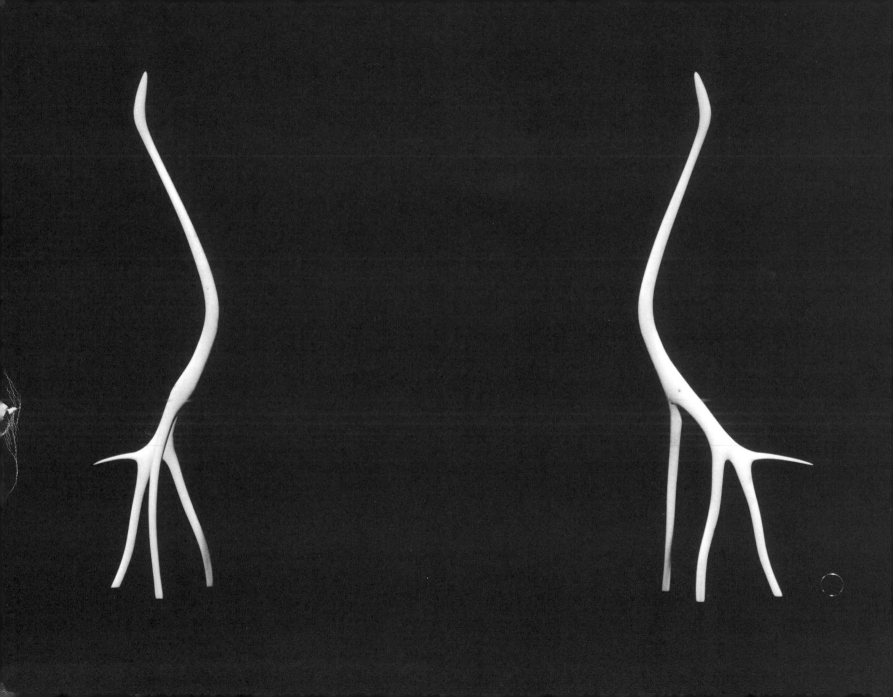

GIRAFFE
DEVELOPMENT DETAILS

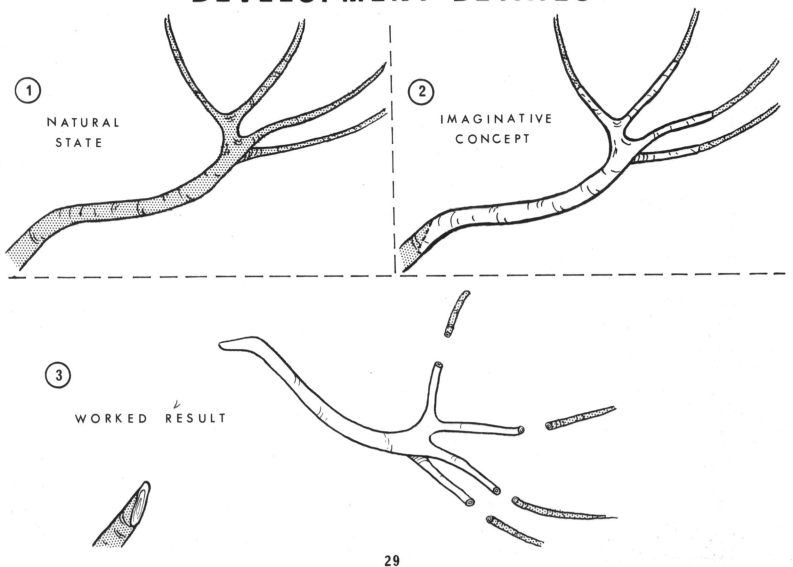

① NATURAL STATE

② IMAGINATIVE CONCEPT

③ WORKED RESULT

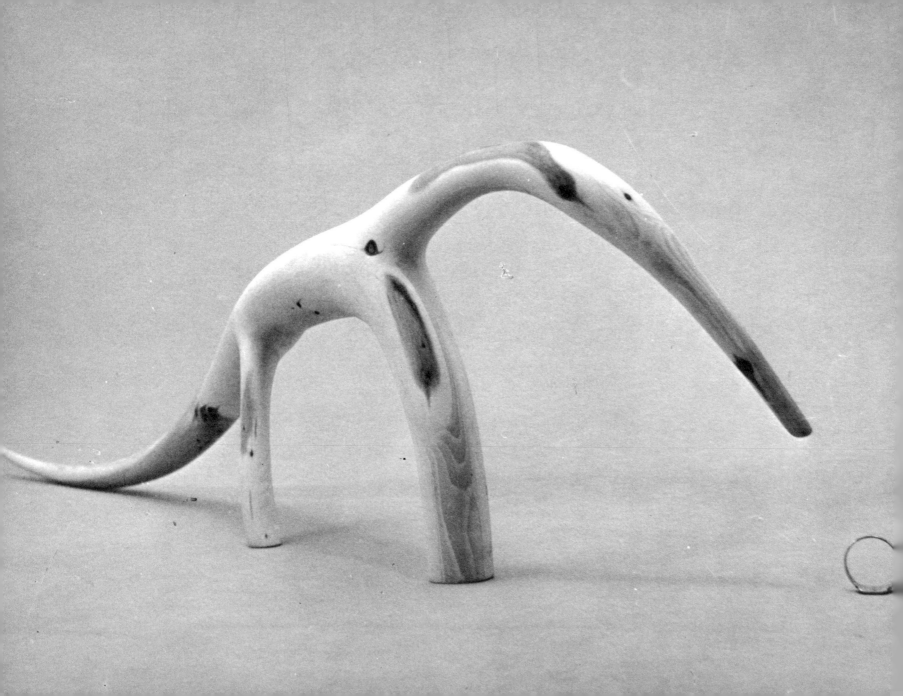

ANT-EATER
DEVELOPMENT DETAILS

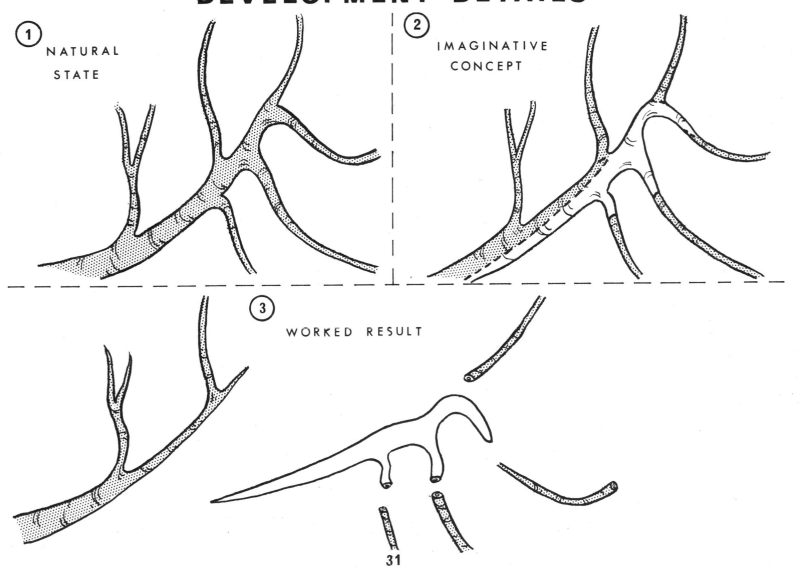

① NATURAL STATE

② IMAGINATIVE CONCEPT

③ WORKED RESULT

31

ANTELOPE
DEVELOPMENT DETAILS

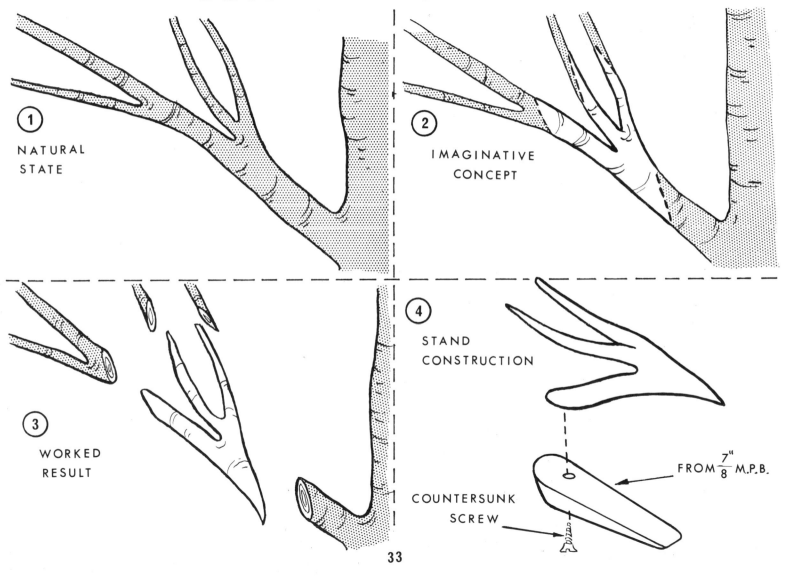

① NATURAL STATE

② IMAGINATIVE CONCEPT

③ WORKED RESULT

④ STAND CONSTRUCTION

COUNTERSUNK SCREW

FROM $\frac{7''}{8}$ M.P.B.

33

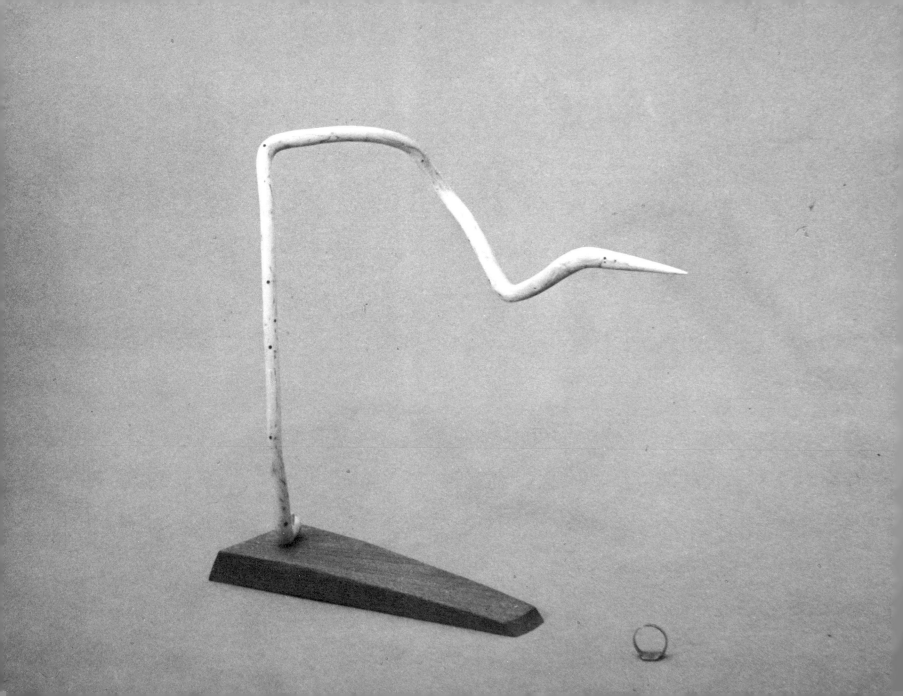

SNAKE
DEVELOPMENT DETAILS

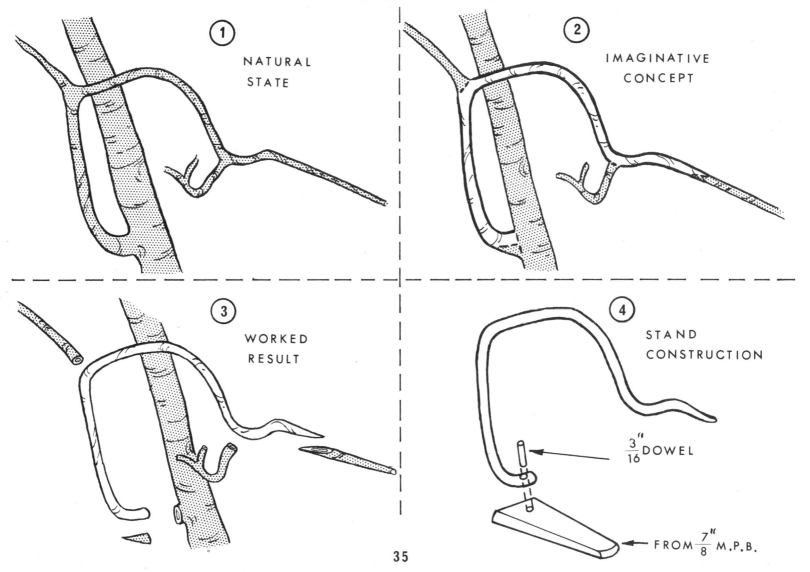

① NATURAL STATE

② IMAGINATIVE CONCEPT

③ WORKED RESULT

④ STAND CONSTRUCTION

$\frac{3''}{16}$ DOWEL

FROM $\frac{7''}{8}$ M.P.B.

35

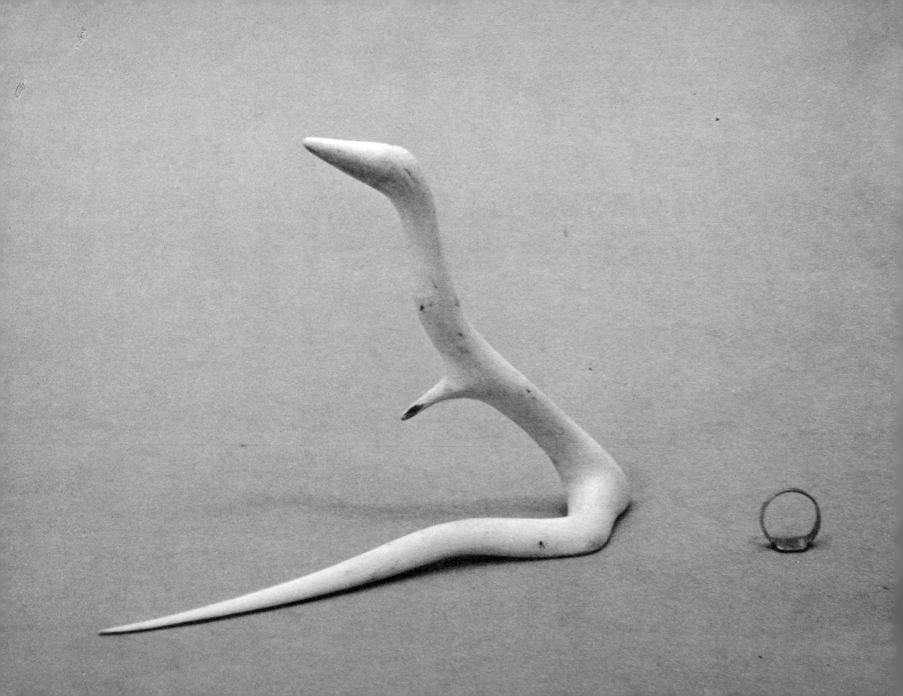

KANGAROO
DEVELOPMENT DETAILS

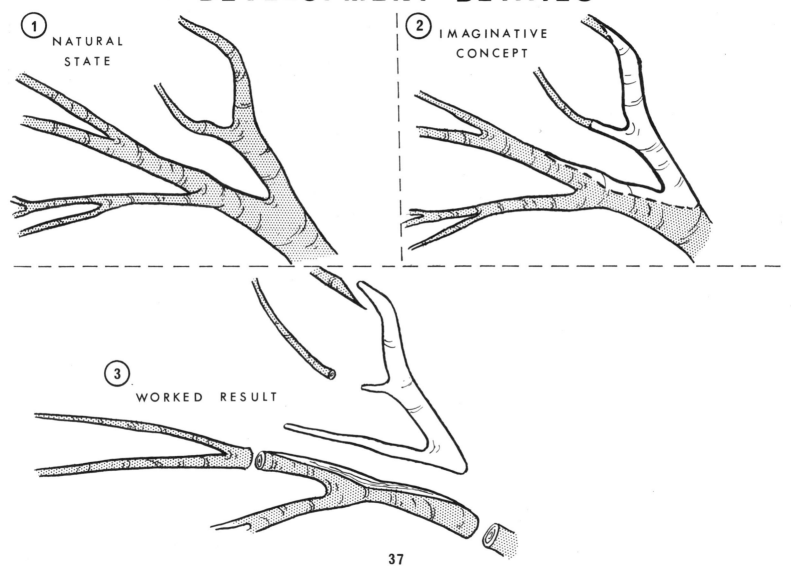

1 NATURAL
STATE

2 IMAGINATIVE
CONCEPT

3 WORKED RESULT

KIWI'S HEAD
DEVELOPMENT DETAILS

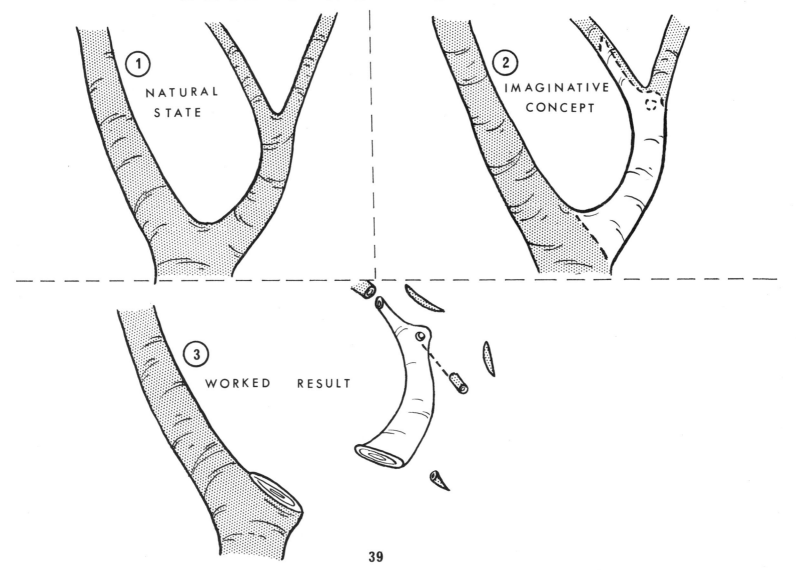

① NATURAL STATE

② IMAGINATIVE CONCEPT

③ WORKED RESULT

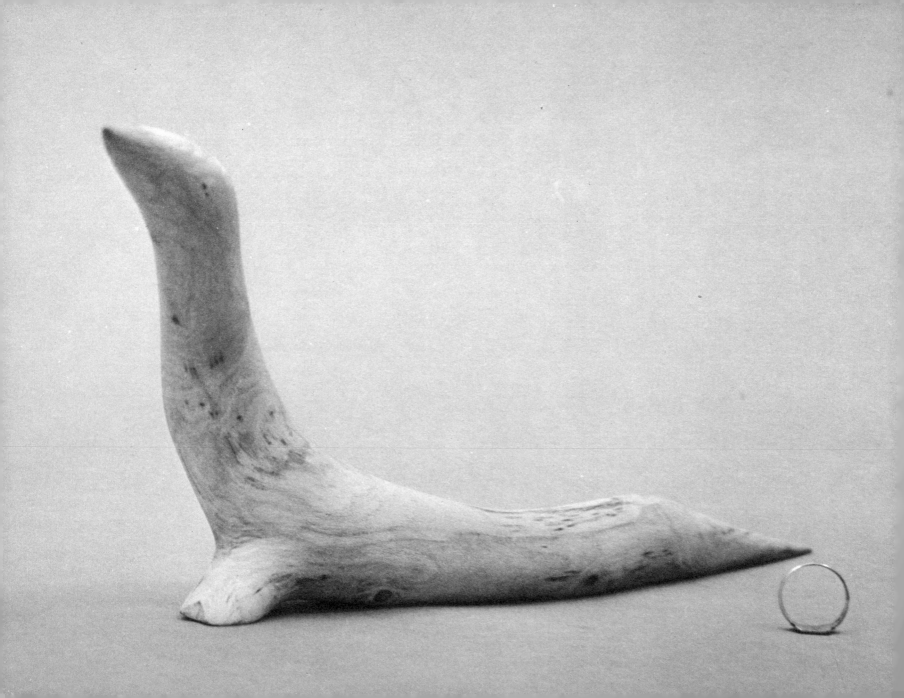

SEAL
DEVELOPMENT DETAILS

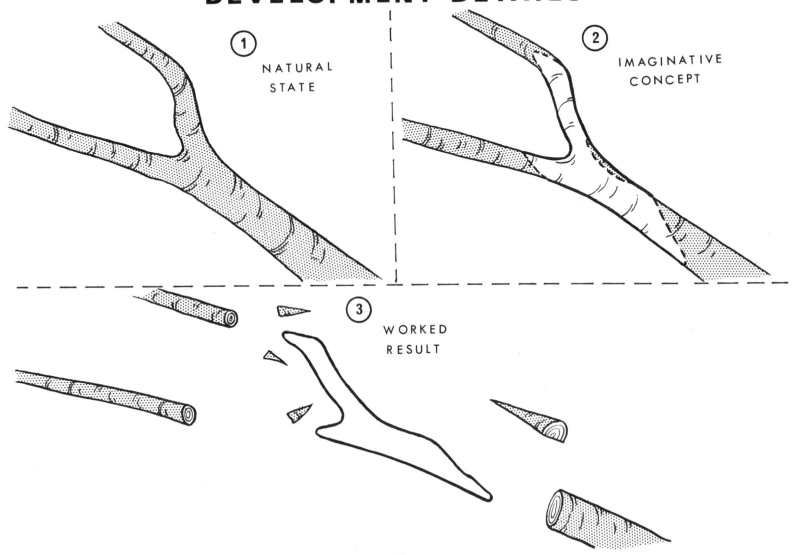

① NATURAL STATE

② IMAGINATIVE CONCEPT

③ WORKED RESULT

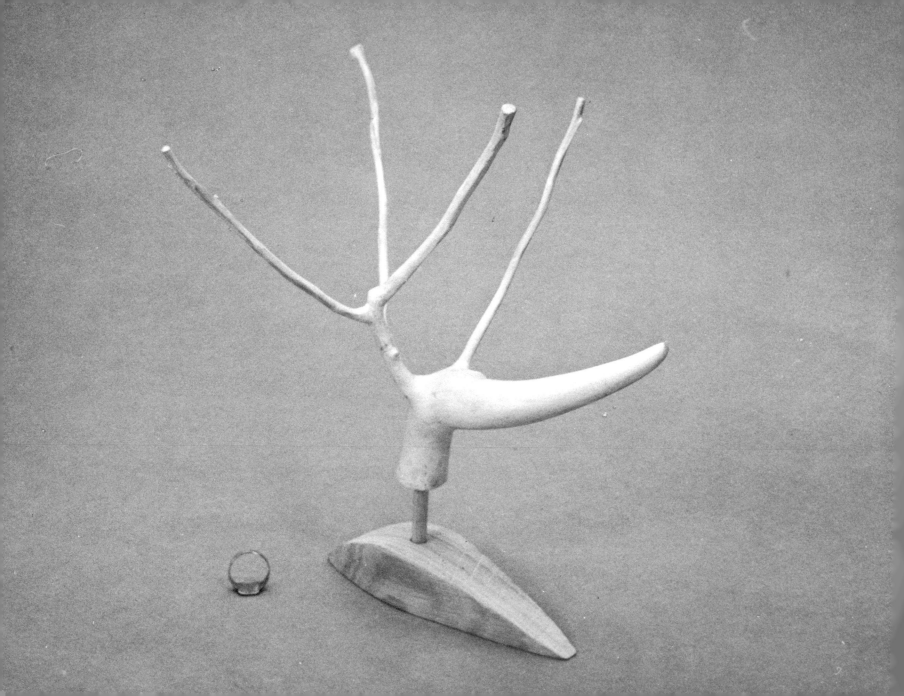

STAG'S HEAD
DEVELOPMENT DETAILS

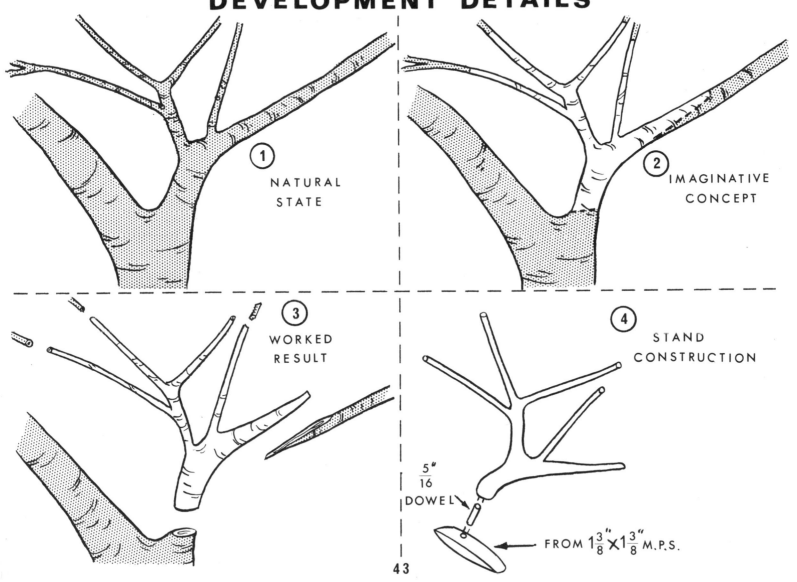

① NATURAL STATE

② IMAGINATIVE CONCEPT

③ WORKED RESULT

④ STAND CONSTRUCTION

$\frac{5}{16}"$ DOWEL

FROM $1\frac{3}{8}" \times 1\frac{3}{8}"$ M.P.S.

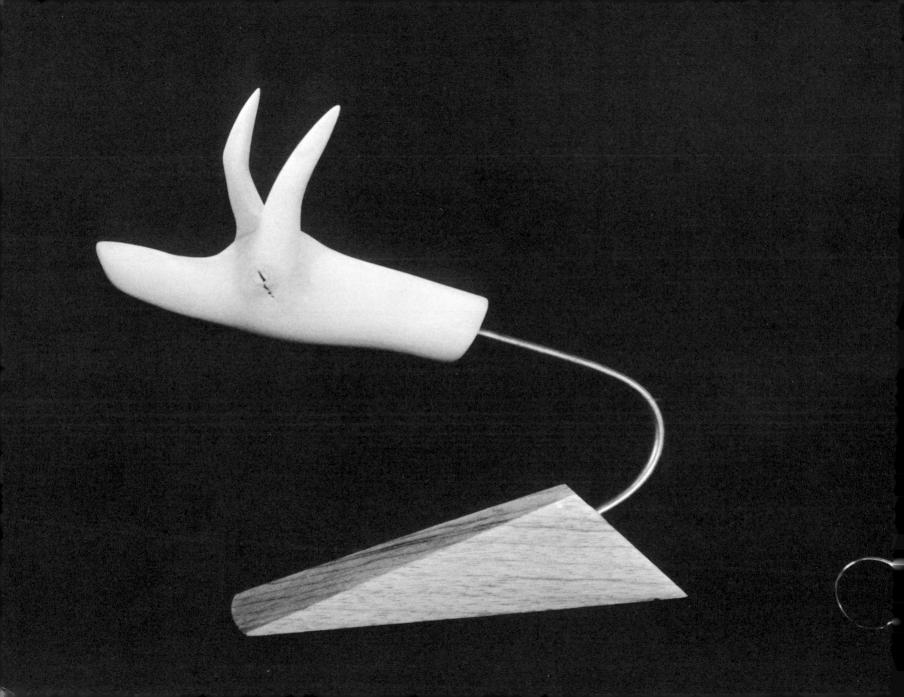

BULL'S HEAD
DEVELOPMENT DETAILS

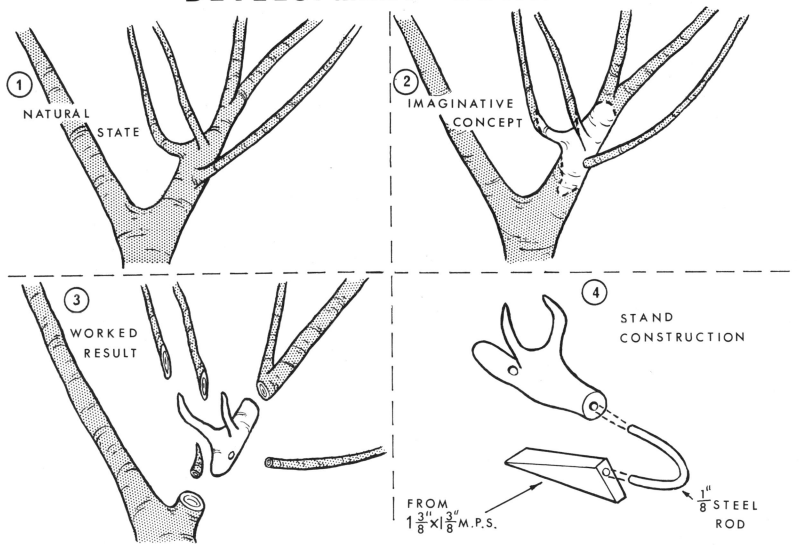

① NATURAL STATE

② IMAGINATIVE CONCEPT

③ WORKED RESULT

④ STAND CONSTRUCTION

FROM $1\frac{3}{8}'' \times 1\frac{3}{8}''$ M.P.S.

$\frac{1}{8}''$ STEEL ROD

RABBIT'S HEAD
DEVELOPMENT DETAILS

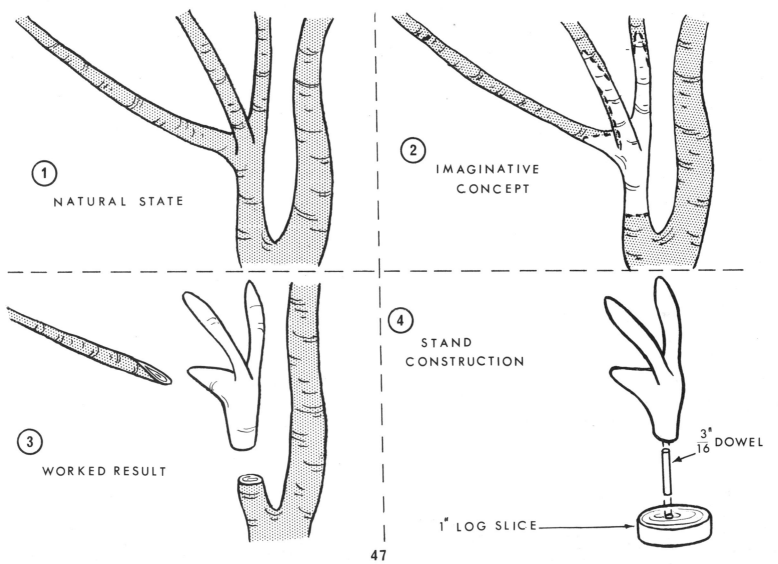

① NATURAL STATE

② IMAGINATIVE CONCEPT

③ WORKED RESULT

④ STAND CONSTRUCTION

$\frac{3"}{16}$ DOWEL

1" LOG SLICE

47

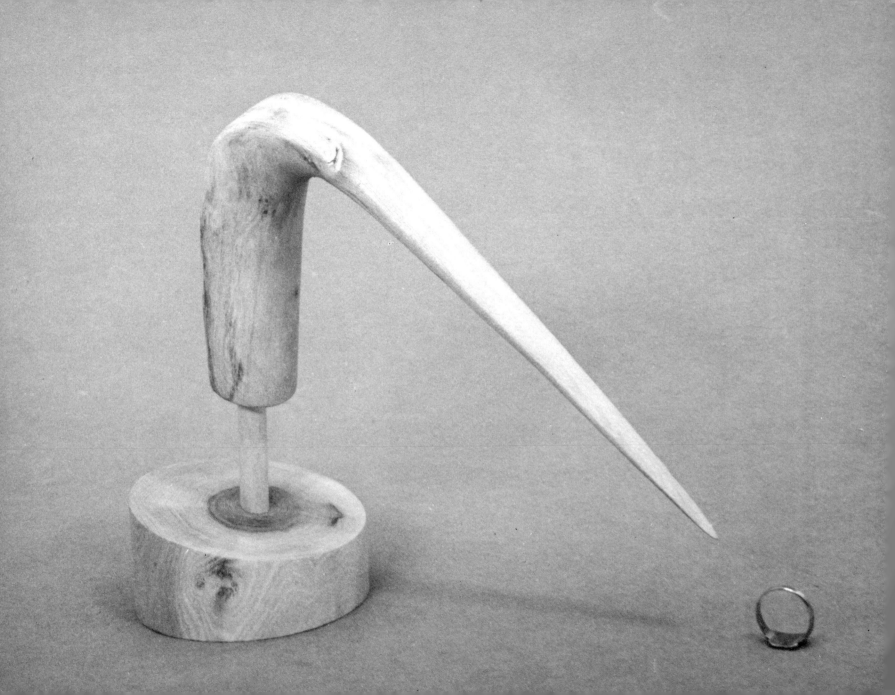

STORK'S HEAD
DEVELOPMENT DETAILS

(1) NATURAL STATE

(2) IMAGINATIVE CONCEPT

(3) WORKED RESULT

(4) STAND CONSTRUCTION

$\frac{5}{16}$" DOWEL

$3\frac{1}{2}$" LOG SLICE

49

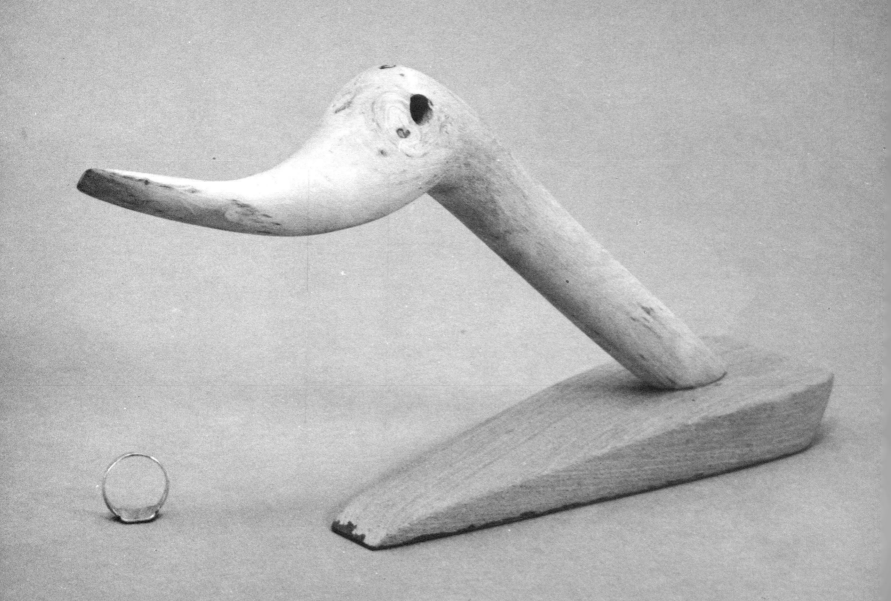

DUCK'S HEAD
DEVELOPMENT DETAILS

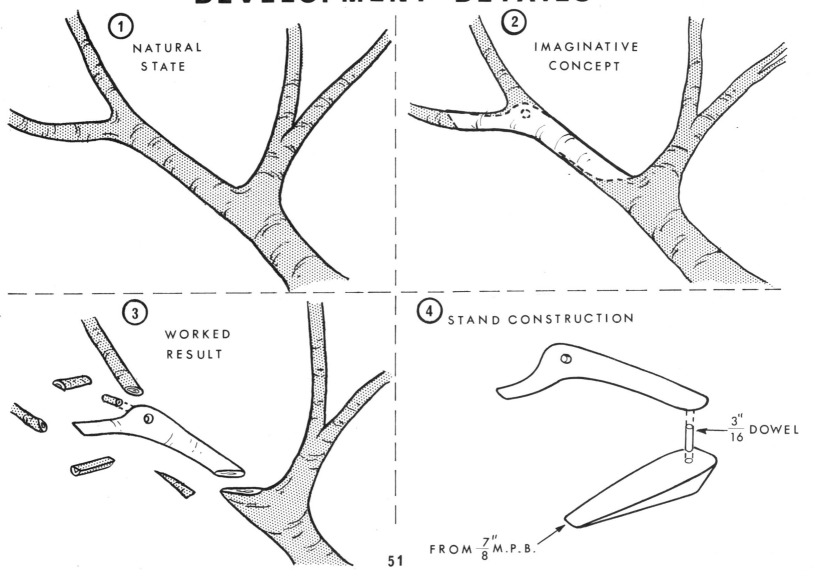

① NATURAL STATE

② IMAGINATIVE CONCEPT

③ WORKED RESULT

④ STAND CONSTRUCTION

$\frac{3"}{16}$ DOWEL

FROM $\frac{7"}{8}$ M.P.B.

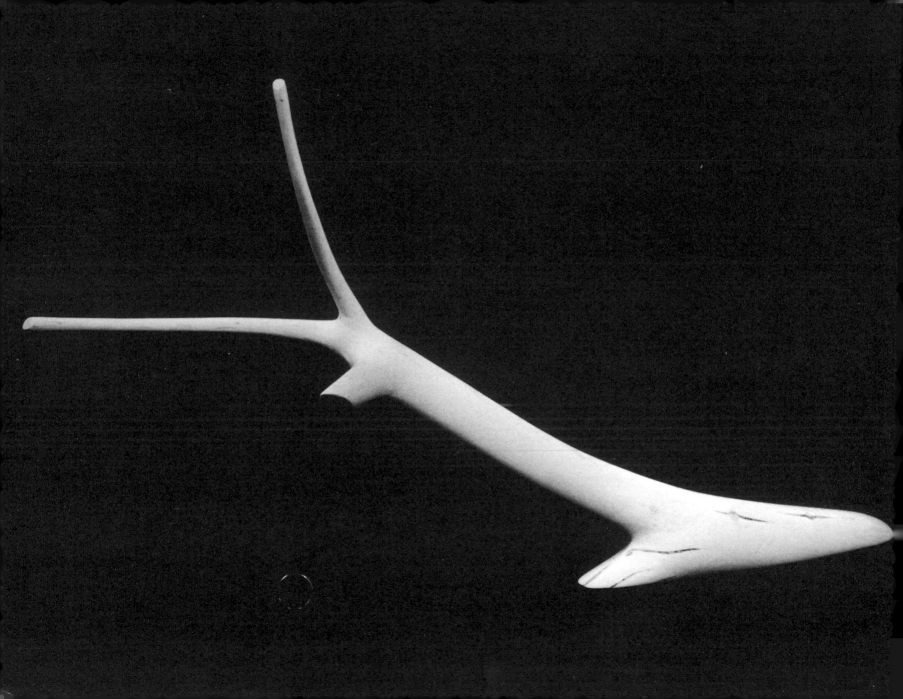

SNAIL
DEVELOPMENT DETAILS

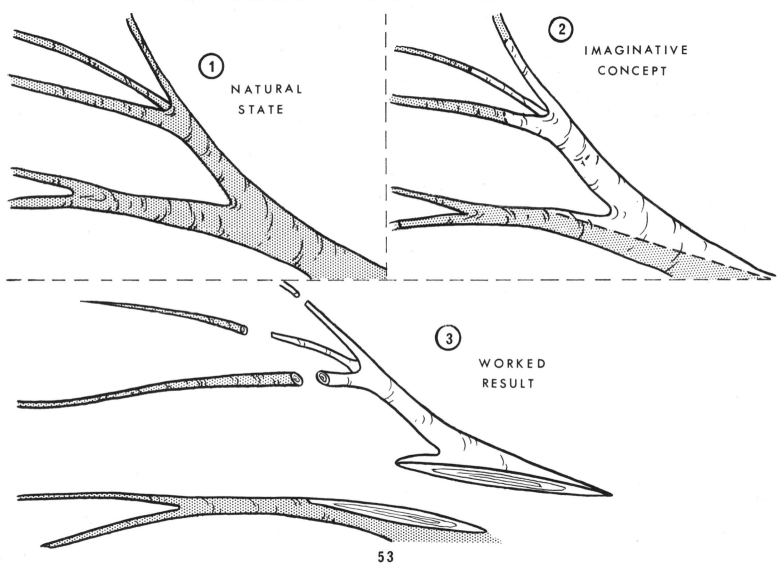

(1) NATURAL STATE

(2) IMAGINATIVE CONCEPT

(3) WORKED RESULT

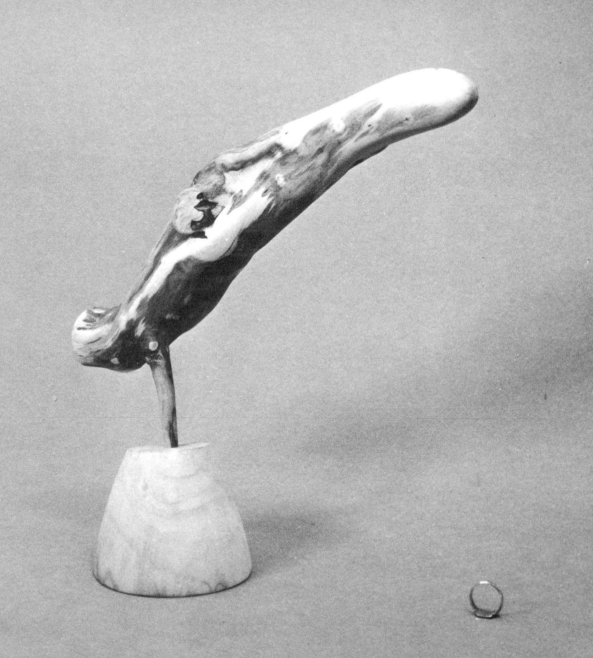

CAMEL'S HEAD
DEVELOPMENT DETAILS

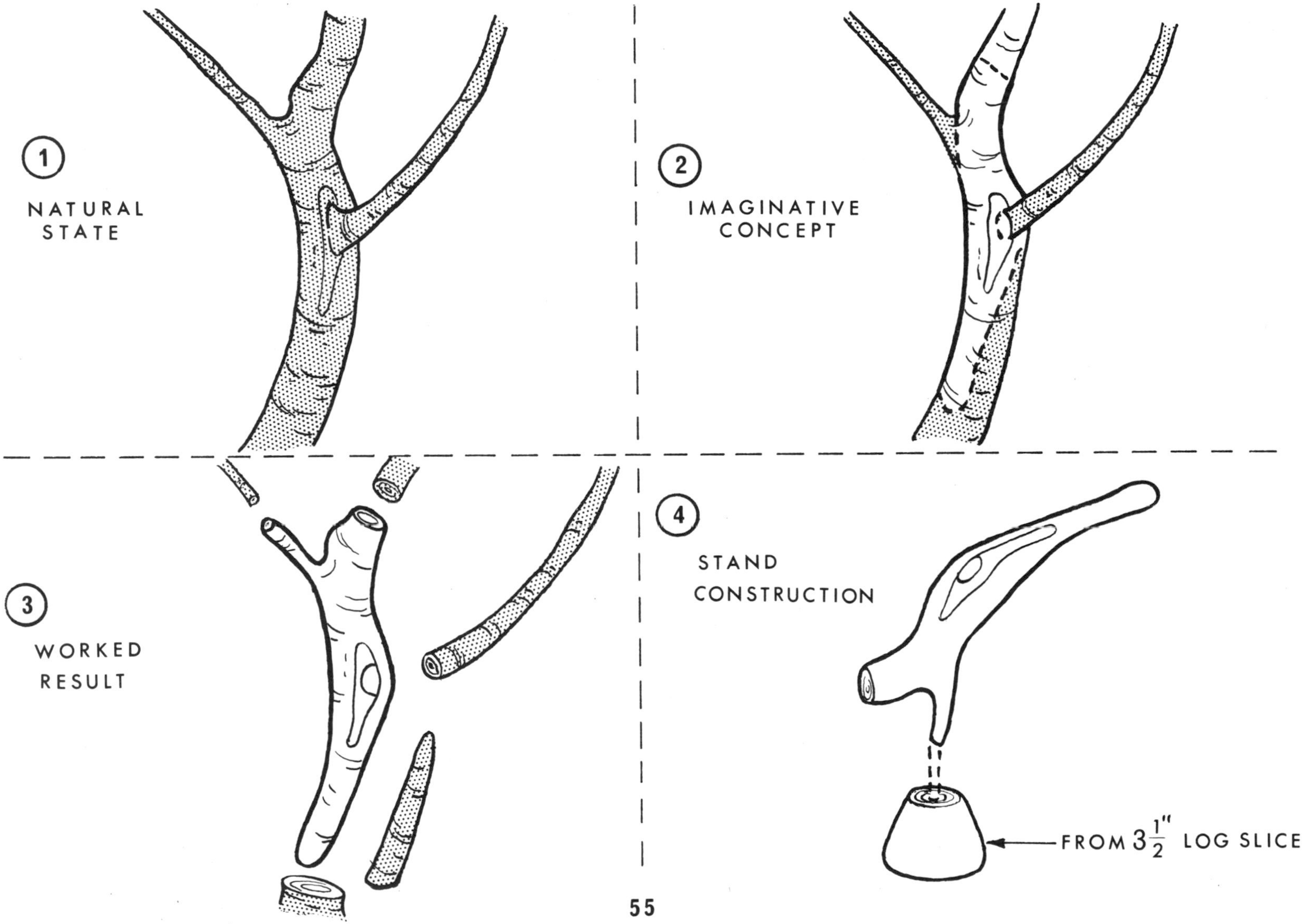

① NATURAL
STATE

② IMAGINATIVE
CONCEPT

③ WORKED
RESULT

④ STAND
CONSTRUCTION

FROM $3\frac{1}{2}''$ LOG SLICE

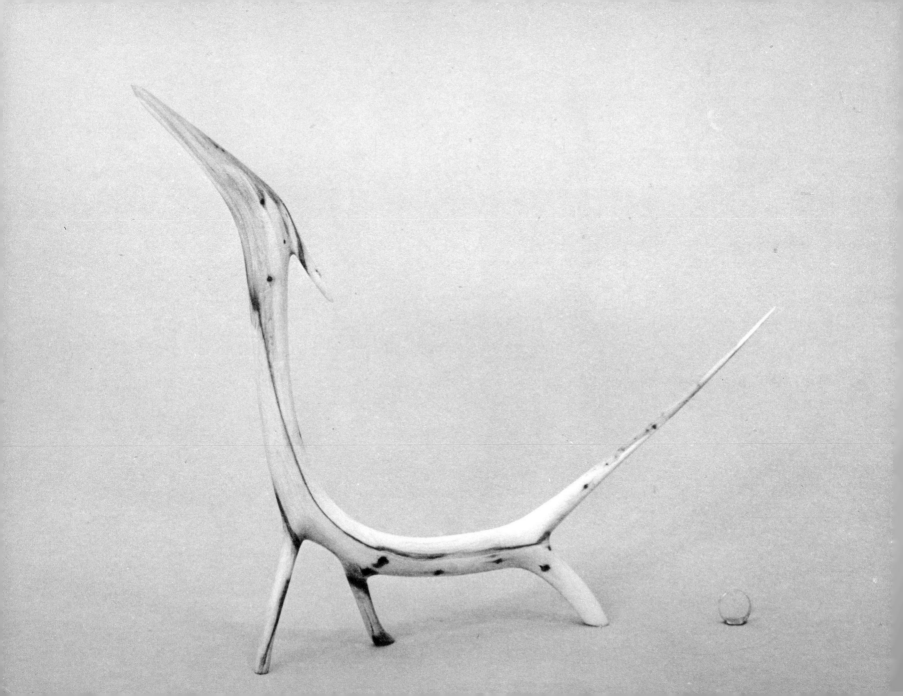

DACHSHUND
DEVELOPMENT DETAILS

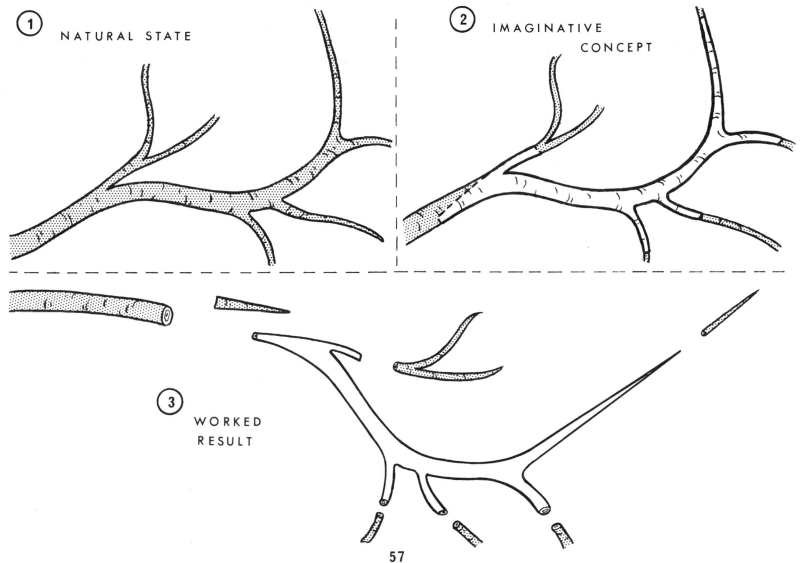

① NATURAL STATE

② IMAGINATIVE CONCEPT

③ WORKED RESULT

57

SUBMARINE
DEVELOPMENT DETAILS

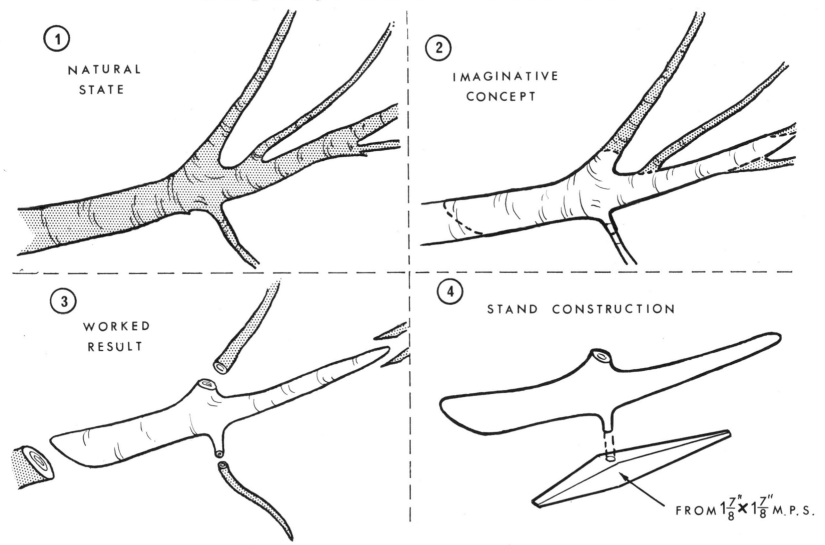

① NATURAL STATE

② IMAGINATIVE CONCEPT

③ WORKED RESULT

④ STAND CONSTRUCTION

FROM $1\frac{7}{8}$" $\times$ $1\frac{7}{8}$" M.P.S.

JET
DEVELOPMENT DETAILS

① NATURAL STATE

② IMAGINATIVE CONCEPT

③ WORKED RESULT

④ STAND CONSTRUCTION

FROM $2\frac{3}{8}'' \times 2\frac{3}{8}''$ M P S

$\frac{1}{8}''$ STEEL ROD

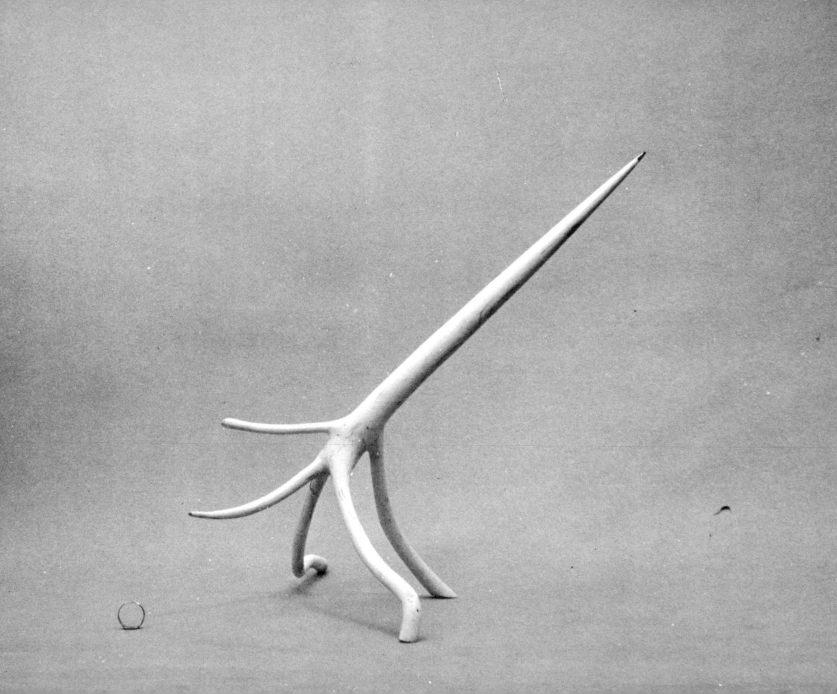

ROCKET
DEVELOPMENT DETAILS

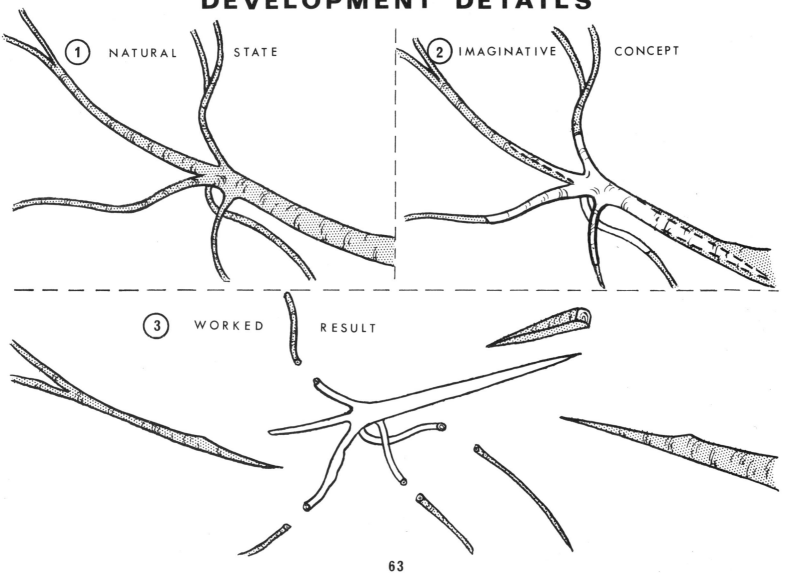

① NATURAL STATE

② IMAGINATIVE CONCEPT

③ WORKED RESULT

63

ANGEL FISH
DEVELOPMENT DETAILS

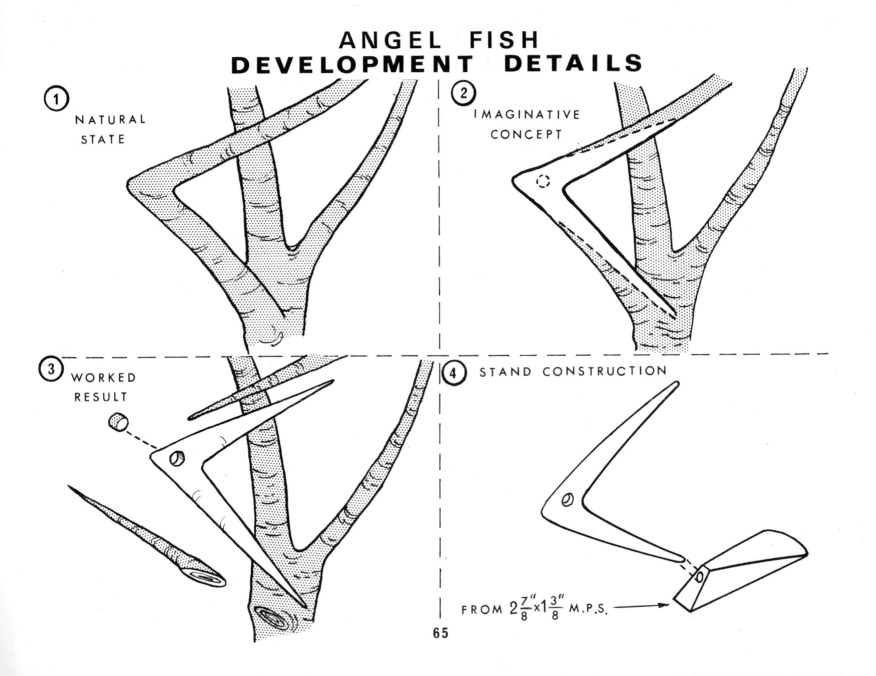

① NATURAL STATE

② IMAGINATIVE CONCEPT

③ WORKED RESULT

④ STAND CONSTRUCTION

FROM $2\frac{7}{8}'' \times 1\frac{3}{8}''$ M.P.S.

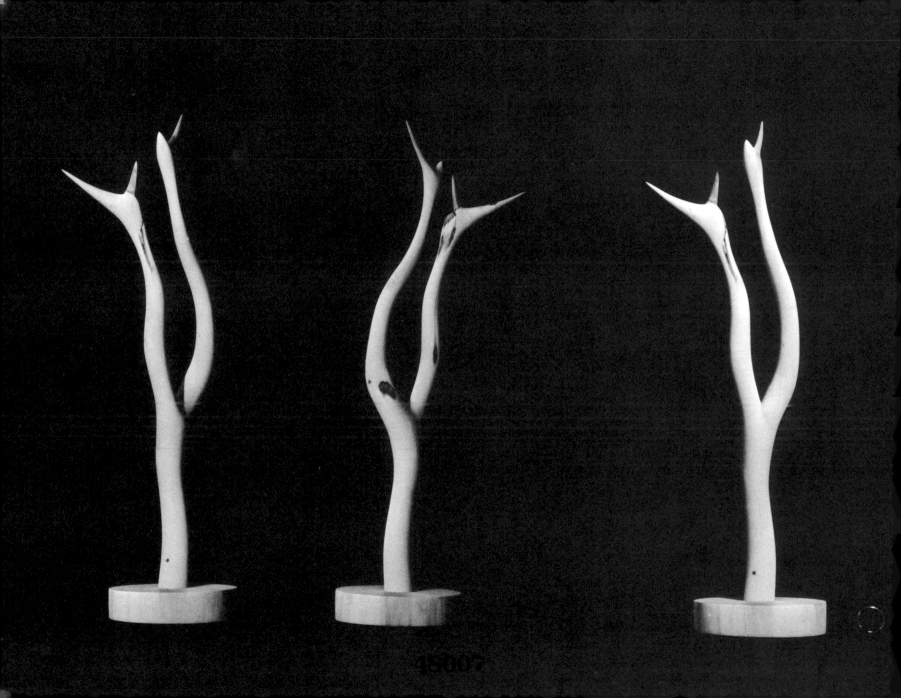

48007

BIRDS
DEVELOPMENT DETAILS

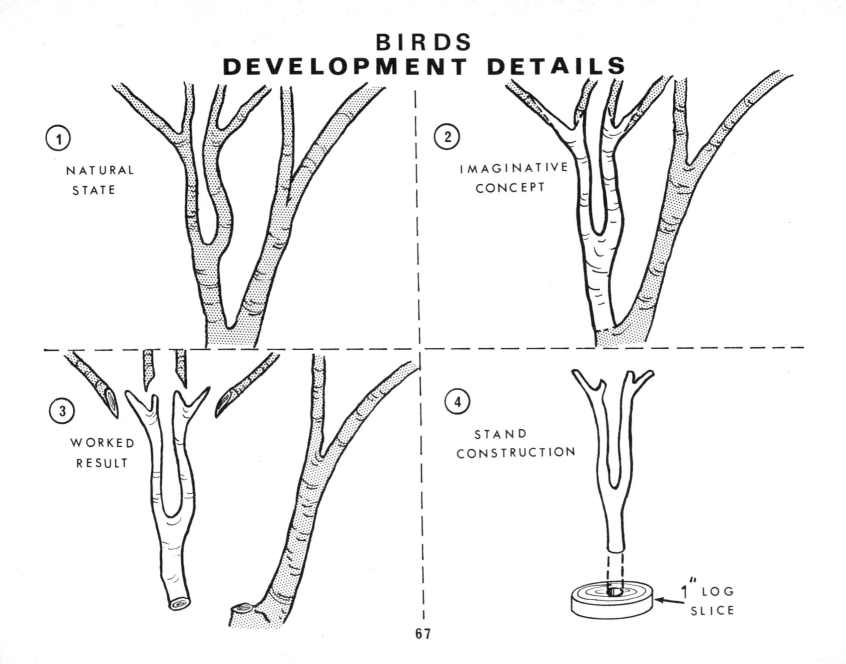

1 NATURAL STATE

2 IMAGINATIVE CONCEPT

3 WORKED RESULT

4 STAND CONSTRUCTION

1" LOG SLICE

MAN AND LOG
DEVELOPMENT DETAILS

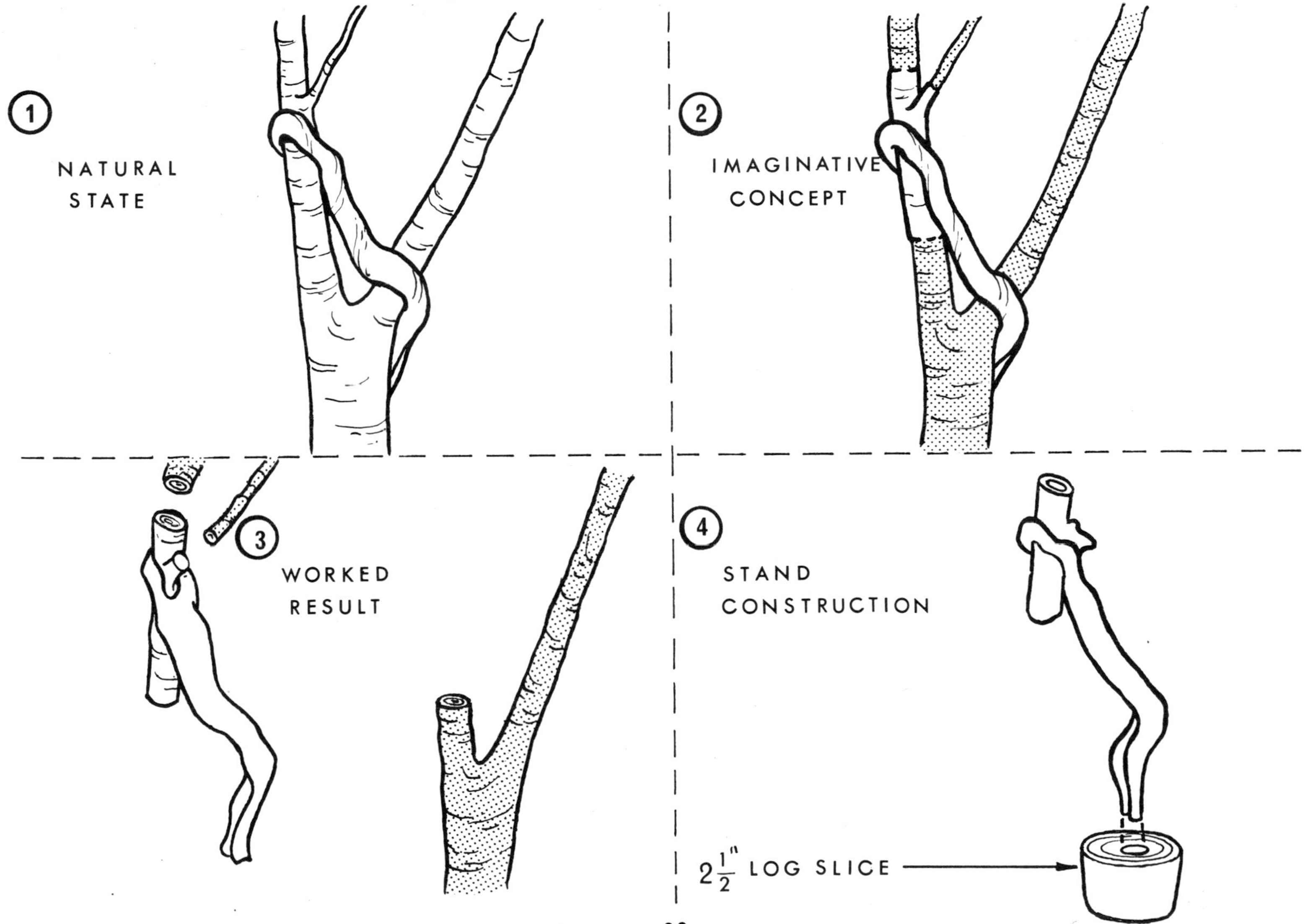

① NATURAL
STATE

② IMAGINATIVE
CONCEPT

③ WORKED
RESULT

④ STAND
CONSTRUCTION

$2\frac{1}{2}"$ LOG SLICE ⟶

SKELETON WORKING GUIDE

① FIRST GAIN OFFICIAL PERMISSION TO SAW 'RAW SCULPTURES'
FROM TREES WHICH ARE TO BE FELLED
OR FELLED BRANCHES.

<u>NOTE</u>

OLD DRY ONES ARE BEST AS THEY WORK EASILY
AND DO NOT TEND TO CRACK OPEN SO MUCH AS
WET ONES.

SKELETON WORKING GUIDE

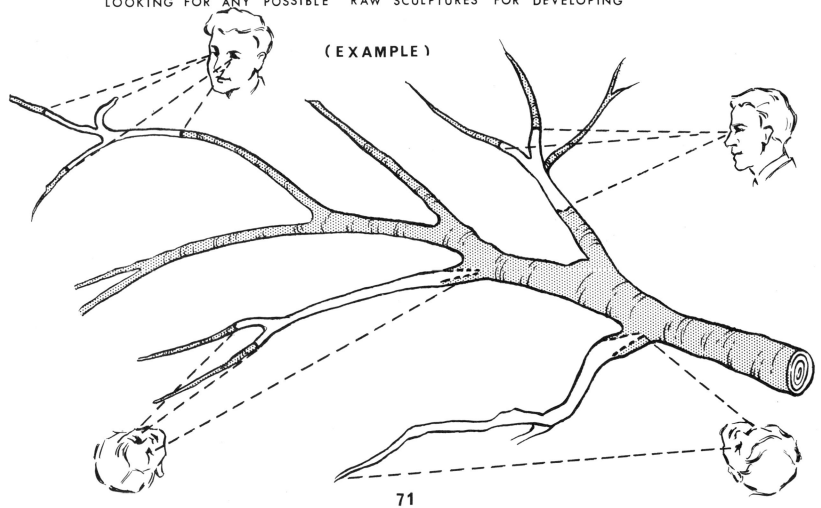

(2) WALK AROUND THE BRANCHES ETC; VIEWING AT DIFFERENT ANGLES

LOOKING FOR ANY POSSIBLE RAW SCULPTURES FOR DEVELOPING

(EXAMPLE)

71

SKELETON WORKING GUIDE

③ SAW OFF THE RAW SCULPTURES ROUGHLY TO SIZE

(EXAMPLES)

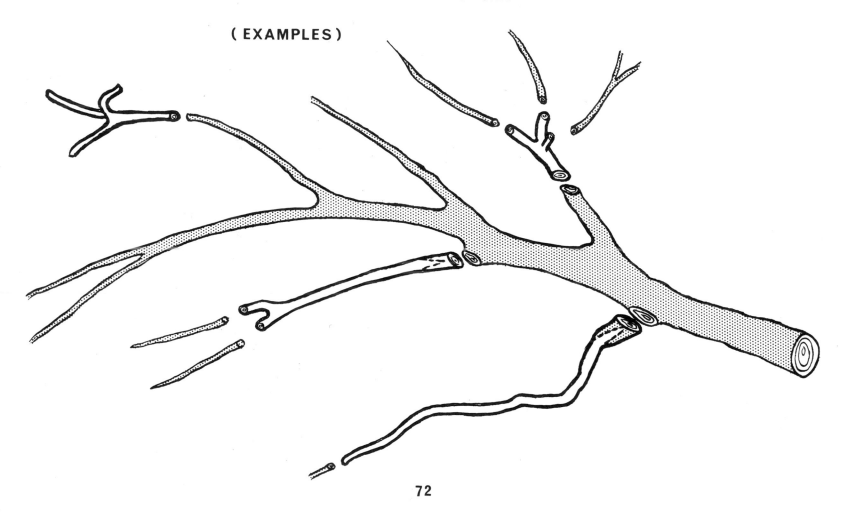

SKELETON WORKING GUIDE

④

TAKE TO SCHOOL OR HOME

THEN CAREFULLY EXAMINE

YOUR RAW SCULPTURE

(EXAMPLE)

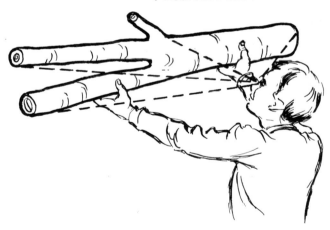

⑤

MARK AND SAW OFF

ANY UNDESIRABLE

LARGE LUMPS

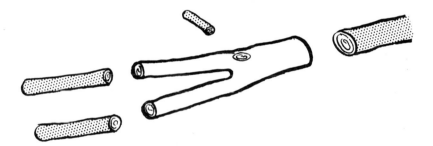

SKELETON WORKING GUIDE

⑥ PEEL OFF THE BARK WHERE
NECESSARY WITH A KNIFE.

⑦ USING THE MOST APPROPRIATE TOOLS
DEVELOP THE SHAPE BY MARKING OUT
AND REMOVING SURPLUS WOOD WITH A
SPOKESHAVE, SURFORM, MEDIUM
CUTTING WOOD RASP, RIFFLER,
FILEMASTER, GOUGE ETC.

Note: It is unwise to allow Junior School children to use gouges.

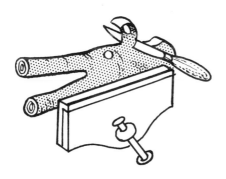

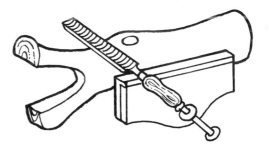

74

SKELETON WORKING GUIDE

NOTE

IF YOU FIND THE WOOD IS VERY WET AND DIFFICULT TO WORK,
STORE IN A SHED OR TEMPERATE ROOM UNTIL IT IS POSSIBLE TO
WORK WITHOUT THE TOOLS BEING CLOUTED UP BY WET SAWDUST
AND SHAVINGS.

(8) FINISH OFF WITH FINE CUTTING
WOOD FILES AND RIFFLERS

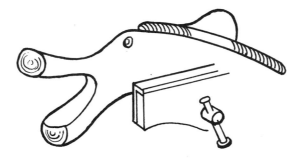

NOTE

IF THOUGHT APPROPRIATE
BORE OR GOUGE EYE HOLES AND
SAW OR GOUGE MOUTH SLITS

SKELETON WORKING GUIDE

⑨ IF A STAND IS REQUIRED, SKETCH FULL SIZED OUTLINES OF
YOUR CARVINGS AND UNDERNEATH SKETCH VARIOUS TYPES OF
APPROPRIATE STANDS.

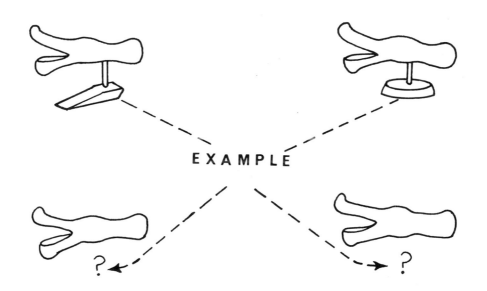

EXAMPLE

SKELETON WORKING GUIDE

⑩ FROM A LOG OR MACHINE PLANED TIMBER, PREPARE, MARK OUT, AND SHAPE THE BASE OF THE STAND WITH THE APPROPRIATE TOOLS.

E X A M P L E

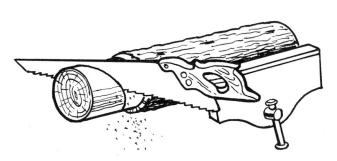

SKELETON WORKING GUIDE

(11) ARRANGE WOOD DOWELS OR THIN STEEL RODS OF VARYING DIAMETER BEHIND THE TOP AND BASE.

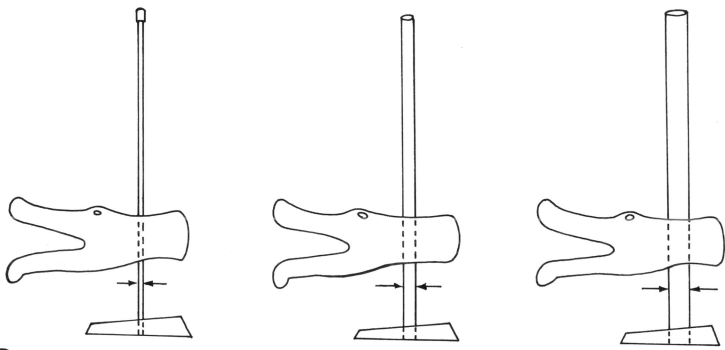

(12) CONSIDER AND CHOOSE THE WOOD DOWEL OR THIN STEEL ROD WHICH LOOKS RIGHT, THEN MARK THE MOST APPROPRIATE BORING POSITIONS IN TOP AND THE BASE.

SKELETON WORKING GUIDE

⑬

FIND A BIT THAT WILL BORE
A SUITABLY TIGHT FITTING HOLE
FOR YOUR CHOSEN SIZE DOWEL
AND SIZE BY TEST BORING
IN A WASTE NOGGIN.

⑭ THEN BORE SUITABLE
DEPTH HOLES IN TOP
AND BASE.

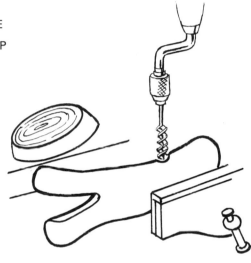

⑮

WORK OUT, MARK, AND SAW
TO LENGTH THE WOOD DOWEL
OR THIN STEEL ROD.

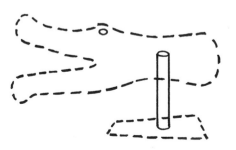

SKELETON WORKING GUIDE

(16)

CLEAN THOROUGHLY
WITH M2 GLASS PAPER.

(17)

CONSTRUCT

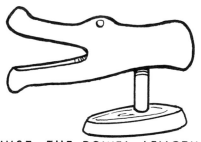

(18)

IF THOUGHT APPROPRIATE
APPLY A SUITABLE FINISH
(POLISH ETC.)

ADJUST THE DOWEL LENGTH
IF NECESSARY

FOR THIS TYPE OF SCULPTURE

THE FOLLOWING TOOLS ARE RECOMMENDED

FOR THEIR SUITABILITY AND QUALITY

FOR HEAVY LOG SAWING

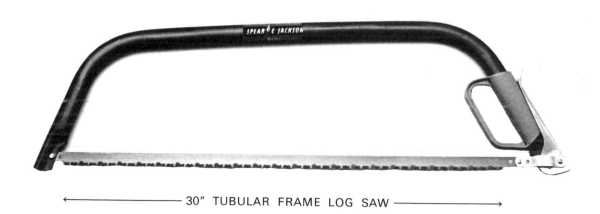

← 30" TUBULAR FRAME LOG SAW →

(Spear and Jackson Ltd, Sheffield)

FOR GENERAL BRANCH SAWING

← ———————— 22" BLACK PRINCE ———————— →

(Spear and Jackson Ltd, Sheffield)

FOR HEAVY DUTY CURVE SAWING

BEECH BOW SAW

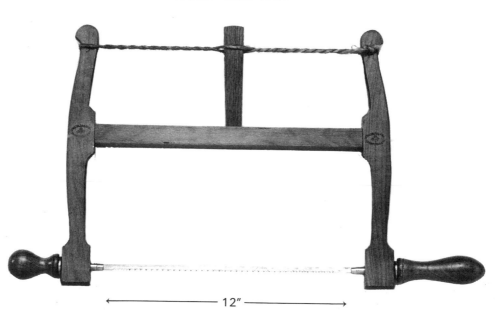

— 12″ —

(William Marples and Sons Ltd, Sheffield)

FOR DELICATE CURVE SAWING

COPING SAW

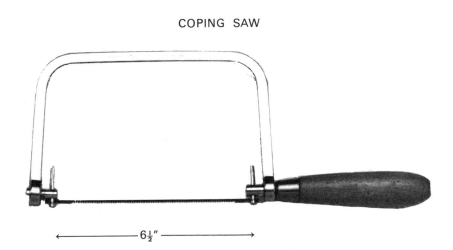

6½"

(William Marples and Sons Ltd, Sheffield)

VICE FOR HOLDING HEAVY WORK

9" HEAVY DUTY BENCH VICE

(C. & J. Hampton Ltd Record Tools, Sheffield)

VICES FOR HOLDING MEDIUM TO SMALL SIZED WORK

6" JUNIOR VICE No. 51

2½" TABLE IMP VICE

(C. & J. Hampton Ltd Record Tools, Sheffield)

87

FOR FLAT BASE SHAPING AND CLEANING UP

ADJUSTABLE METAL SMOOTH PLANE CUTTER WIDTH 2"

$9\frac{3}{4}$"

FOR FINE CURVED BULK SHAPING AND CLEANING UP

FLAT FACE MALLEABLE IRON SPOKESHAVE $2\frac{1}{8}$" CUTTER

(C. & J. Hampton Ltd, Record Tools, Sheffield)

FOR GENERAL ROUGHING OFF

← ——————— 10" HALF-ROUND CABINET RASP ——————— →

FOR GENERAL CLEANING UP

← ——————— 10" HALF-ROUND CABINET FILE ——————— →

(George Barnsley and Sons Ltd, Sheffield)

**THESE SURFORM TOOLS ARE
ESPECIALLY GOOD FOR GENERAL
SHAPING IN SOFT WOODS**

SURFORM BLOCK PLANE No. 111A

SURFORM STANDARD PLANE No. 107A

(Stanley Works Ltd, Sheffield)

SURFORM STANDARD FILE No. 101A

SURFORM ROUND FILE No. 124

(Stanley Works Ltd, Sheffield)

FOR ROUGHING OFF AND CLEANING UP AWKWARD CORNERS

←————— 9" TAPERED HALF-ROUND RIFFLER (ROUGH AND FINE ENDS) ————→

←————— 9" TAPERED ROUND RIFFLER (ROUGH AND FINE ENDS) ————→

←————— 9" TAPERED TRIANGULAR RIFFLER (ROUGH AND FINE ENDS) ————→

(William Marples and Sons Ltd, Sheffield)

FOR SMALL DELICATE WORK

SET OF SIX SMALL-SIZE CARVING TOOLS No. 153

FOR GENERAL WORK

SET OF SIX MEDIUM-SIZE CARVING TOOLS No. 152

(William Marples and Sons Ltd, Sheffield)

HEAVY DUTY GOUGES FOR
ROUGHING OFF AND A GOUGED FINISH

CARVERS MALLET

LONG POD
GOUGE
No. 6 1½″ WIDE

CURVED
GOUGE
No. 17 1¼″ WIDE

FISH TAIL
GOUGE
No. 3 1½″ WIDE

(Stormont Archer Ltd, Sheffield)

94

DUAL PURPOSE TOOLS FOR LARGE SURFACE ROUGHING OFF AND CLEANING UP

TRIMMATOOL

FILEMASTER

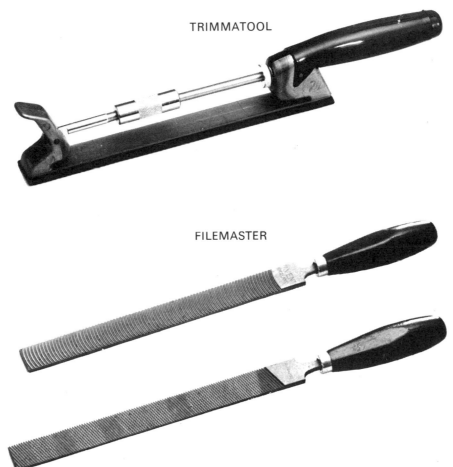

(Aven Works, Maltby, Yorkshire)

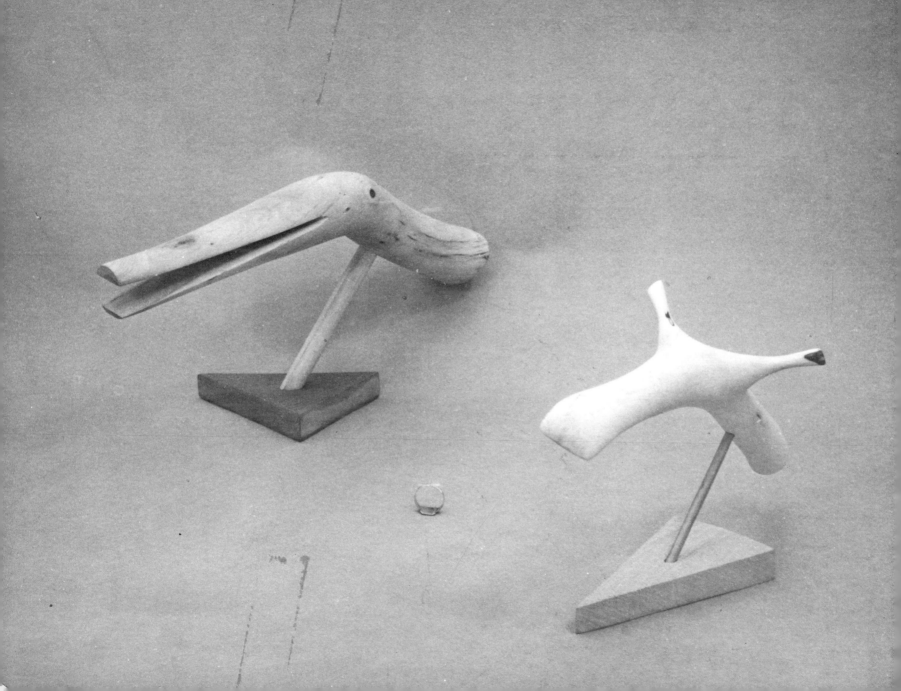